Thee Poetz Promise To be Dope

Vol.
GHETTO POETRY BY BELLA MARTRICE
II

ISBN 978-1-956534-11-5

Thank you to POOR Press team for design and copy-editing.

Cover design by Ndi Filmz
Artwork by Tristen Hornstein and Roger Moore

**A POOR Press Publication © 2024 Bella Martrice Candler.
All Rights Reserved.**

POOR Press is a poor and indigenous people-led press dedicated to publishing the books and scholarship of youth, adults, and elders in poverty locally and globally.

www.poormagazine.org
www.poorpress.net

When it was okay to b u
You there quietly
Spinning sticky webs
With perfectly crafted
Geometric shapes
Mimicking the
Harmless beauty
Of snow flakes
With the meticulousness
Of a spider and seamstress
Quietness is often mistaken
As peaceful
You there building a magnetic
Force field
Laying brick by brick quietly
Being quite is often confused
With patient
Just keep spinning...
To b continued

The sun bats its last rays
Like lashes
A temporary goodbye
To the sky
My daughter finishes her homework
Yet
I have yet to run with the wind
Barefoot..
Halo of dark brown unruly curls
Eye fixated on nothingness
Thoughts orbiting
Like rings on Saturn
Hoping rage doesn't return
Violence bubbling within
Like volcanic matter
I can feel pulsating
My childish id
Impulsive self gratifying
Yes.. I forgot to run with the wind

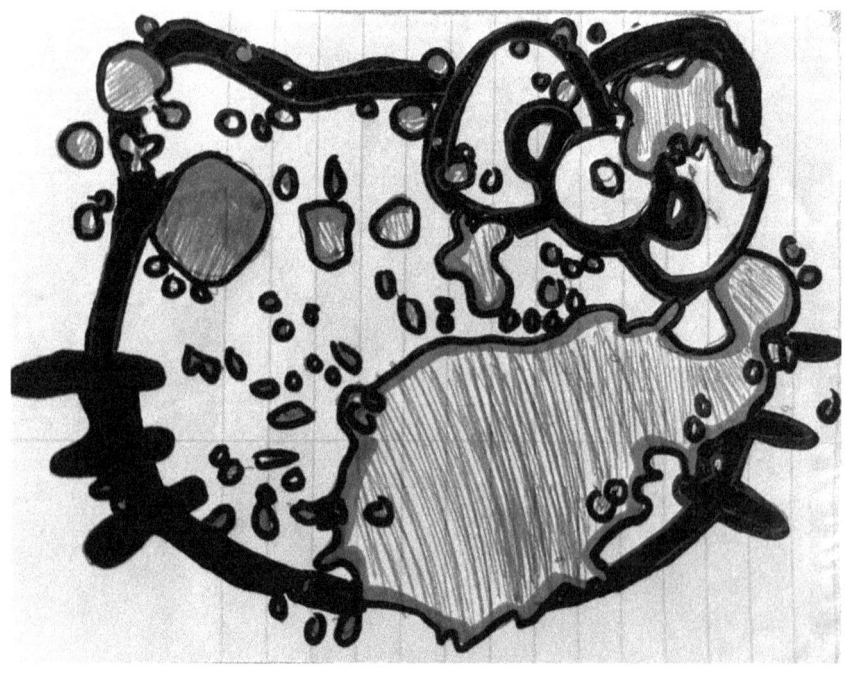

art by Tristen Hornstein

Tasteless imperfection
Pointing fingers
Nit pickings
Wanting to put witches
Back on burning crosses
Once we conjure power
Why are you afraid??
Are you not entertained??
I see you nonchalantly
Give atrophy to your demon
What God don't you believe in?
How do you segregate Goddesses
And Gods
But praise Rosa parks
For not giving up her seat
You like dead power
Past tense context
You like to admire
Revolution
Evolution
But there
U
Are dilution
You
Cotton picking brain
Your spirit ball in chain
As I astro project
To my next
Project
You tryna to convince me
To return to your shackles
You should be a feminist too
Didn't you
Incubate
Beneath
A Black woman's flesh
Was not a Black womb
Your world???
Wasn't a black
Woman's heart beat
Your first instrumental
You heard her tears
Before you felt rain
Have you not tasted
A black woman's blood
When you came bursting out
Of her womb..
Do you want to return?
You should be a feminist!!
Ya grandmother's grandmother's
Great great granny
Prayed for you
Slaved fa you
Yes.. Literally
Slaved for you
And fucked for you
Accepted rape as a
Casualty of this earthly war
Rape and Prostitution
Are Slavery's friendly fire
Shots fired
Black women
Please stand thee fuck up
#lemonaide

Poverty's Child (Eric I)
For Eric D. Phillips Jr

Skin unblemished (to me)
Stretch marks around your biceps
Is body decoration
that takes you physically
Up two notches from the average nigga (I Feel it)
It makes you more exquisite
Your scars are hieroglyphs
Provoke questions
Pertaining to your personal history
Your existence
I'm gonna ask questions
For I dont believe you are stereotypically
"A Nigga "
Visual artifacts
Of how you been livin
You been shot
Like Pac
By niggaz on your block tryna rob
While your momz n pops was smokin rocks
No tears, you were huggin the block
Caught the bus home
when you were shot
No ambulance no cops
No tuition
This is the school of hard knocks
Tell your story
This poems the pilot
reiterating your plot
Og's gave u powder packs
U hid them in ur tube socks
fresh off the block
1st at the beanery line
Ordering pizza
for u and yo hungry potna
your clothes made you povertys child
No fashionista

Guidance counselors gives no guidance
Bus stop fights
Where a boys feeling not honored
So ya boys ego's takin flight
No Hawks
To teach him to truly fly
Gravitation pulls
Umbilical cord yanks him back to the ghetto
Squares think there better
So ummmmm, squares be aware bra...
Magnifying glass on the boys
Whos skin the color of rich soil
Believing what the media say
Will destroy you
I understand your turmoil
Animated chocolate
your skins EXOTIC...
They say the blacker
The berry the sweeter the juice
I say the blacker the man
The richer the soil
from which the Black berry grew
You the truth God made you

Bella's Angel (Eric II)
For Eric D. Phillips Jr.

Immortalize
Thru poetry
Established in 1980
A 80$ Baby
Like me
E Money
A real Bri rite
Nigga

A good man
My friend
Shit
That's my left hand
Right when I'm wrong
If you go left on
Me he address
And correct
It
He my spell check
Check me
He my lefty
Ice me
Wife me
Wedding ring

Told me have a
Nigga come
15 thousand or harder

My nigga
Got murdered
He A martyr
He's been whispering
In the wind
All in my ear
Go smarter
Go harder

My baby daddy
My ex lover

Still
My nigga
My friend
When he
Was in the
Bink
I'd write
Him in
The pen
When he was in the bink
He send me flowers
From the pen
Write my poems
See ima
Poem too
Mirror
My nigga
My stress
My bless
My family my
Friend

Eric gotta
Halo
Wingz n
Thingz
Gods hunters point beast

High powered
Didn't believe
In pimpin
Or hitting
Women
He hate niggaz like
That
Don't fuck
White bitches
Don't like weak
Women
Malcolm x

Thee Enforcer
Enforcement
Gods Ghetto soldier
But now
He's Bella's Angel

My nigga
Eric got a halo

art by Tristen Hornstein

Oppressed

I think the sky
Mimicked
The internal riot
Going on in
All of our minds
But the sky cried
For the egotistical
For the hard hearted
Sister of man
Kind
For babies
Aborted
Who were terminated
Before their first
Breath
For babies
That grew to men
And havent cried
Since
For domestic violence
Victims
Hiding black eyes
Under designer glasses
For domestic violence
Aggressors
Whose guilt
Been eating them up
Since
For little boys
Whos muffled
Cries hasnt escaped
Tear stained pillows
For apologies
Undistributed
For guilty white librals
For racist republicans and
Democrats
For frats
For legitimate and
Illegitimate children
Bastard

For pimps
That hoe
Hoes that pimp
Pimps
Hoez that dont
Have sex
For confused
Socially unconscious
Black girls
Suffering
And distributing
Internalized racism
For latina girls
Who think they
Are better
Than Black women
But have Black daughters
For Black men
Who tell them this
For fat girls
That
Think they eat too much
For skinny girls
That starve
For chubby chasers
Who hide
Their lust and love
For Big girls
For fat boys
Who arent ballin
For the man whose
Job cant keep him
For the educated
Who are overqualified
For the hispanic men
Who buys Black flesh
For oppressed
For BLACK MEN
WHO FEELS
THEIR MOMMAS
ARE BEAUTIFUL

BUT HATE WOMEN
WHO LOOK JUST
LIKE HER
FOR the upper class
For the people
Who are afraid to be called Crazy
Inter generation , sexual, racial
Religious ageist classist, sizeist
Homophobic, anorexic, bloated
Fat and hungry
Skinny and full

Poor and rich
Loveless
Convoluted
Confused
Self segregated
Forced segregated
The far fetched
The few
The in-between
Imbetween
Oppressed

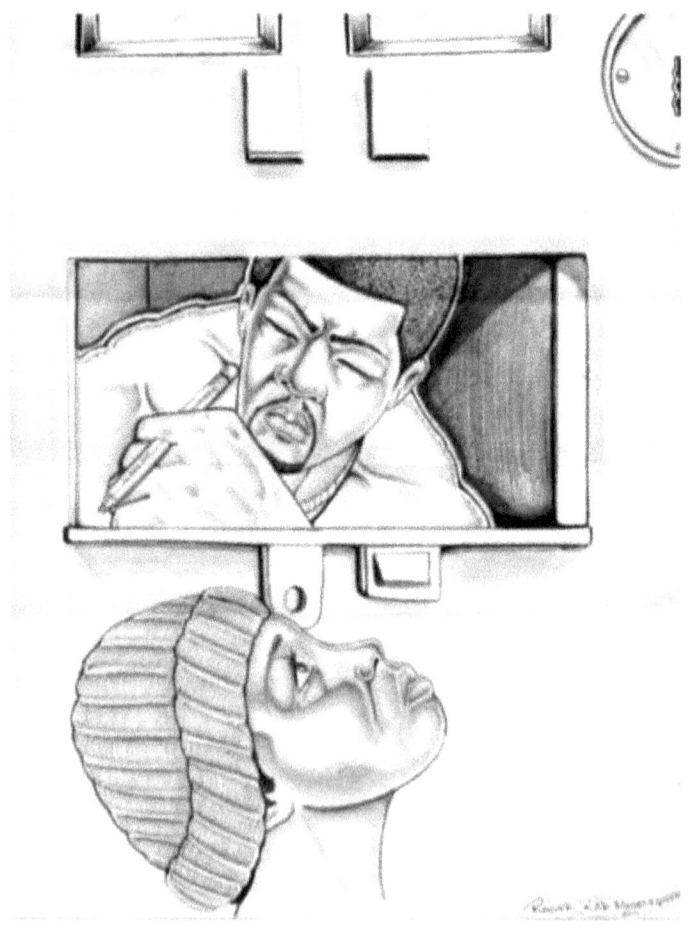

art by Roger Moore

Inspired by my grandmothers death.. RIP Nana

My mind must b hallow
My tears echo
When they hit the back stairs
At my grandmother's house
Loud like
6 light skin, bright skin
Curly haired, wild
Motherless kids
Running down the stairs
Bumpty, jumpin
Berry pickin, kitten catching
Get low n
Fillmoe shit
God knows
We was always into to something
I'm in memory lane
feels like 'I'm traveling through a bent arms vein
fist fights and birthday parties
smoking beedies n bomb
n the lobby
rapping and cappin
our hobbies
finishing Puerto Rican rum In the lobby
dumb niggaz n bitches treating our home
like it's the jets
minor respect
It's only what they could pro ject
They going through the same shit
They was from the projects
Nana yelling
Cane hittin the floor
Demanding the power like Asatta Shakur
So focused on pleasure n war
Not how these "street stripes"
Conflict with our internal décor
failing at being rebellious
I'm rebelling
just an undusted medallion
light barely
Illuminating my talent
Now my tears my instrumental
Pain was, sought, taught n brought
like fine gourmet dishes
or in exchange for neglected intuition
God does those dishes
what we sought
was truly hidden
a fruit forbidden
how does one not give n to the glitter?
I t jus happens
Individual's mis steering children
Disposable pawns
In their agendas
children whose tears are there instrumentals
But, Gold don't glitter
Most wouldn't recognize
Platinum
Call it silver
But diamonds do
Yes they do
Gold shimmered on my neck as an adolescent
Jordans
Mac lip glass on my lips
jerseys and criss cross cuts n my eye brow
Are these reasons fights were projected
Naaa! Maybe an influence
It was way more complex
I would never tolerate a mutha fucka
Taking my shit
After my mother was murdered
Id fight till death
What's next
is bitches with a light skin complex?
I embrace my European descendants

My clothes n soul is vintage
I v been feeling the familiarity
In my earthy pilgrimage
We good…
My father always told me
This is my best learning ground
I didn't understand it then
Like a sphere
shits coming around
we went from, step on a crack
momma gonna break her back
to my niggaz selling crack to mommas
who broke their backs
I can feel emotional under tows n currents
From my niggaz being murdered
To under aged females being
Manipulated to satisfy
Ogs sexual perversions
These were our ghetto excursions
Sometimes I look in mirror
See a mean mug in the mirror
Talk and hear the pain n ghetto in my tenor
wish I could pitch a smooth stone
down The wishing well.
Id wish for a million wishes
Then I remember I would b a girl unwishing
Stuck in never land
I wouldn't be tricey baby 415
jus a girl jus wishing
I had appreciated my memories
Never trading
my insight for wishing
Embracing my intuition

For Maya Angelou

Who will remember her?
Her dreams
A deformed infant
That she nurtured
Whispering promising this baby
Crippled
Ugly
Crying scared
Scarred
From a scraped and battered womb
Still her seed
She whispered
beauty
Grow
Or do you remember the elders
Displeasing mouths
Turned downward like a
Upside down crescent moon
Still her seed
She commanded
With the thunder
In her voice like a santafied
Man of the cloth
High off the holy spirit
Beauty!!
Grow!!!
Mainstreamed
They enticed her to feed this dream
Enfamil discouraged
From the breast
And organic alternatives
You see I never understood
The importance of accepting Jesus
If I had accepted God..
Until my love, my dream
Was of topic in a conversation
As if there was a possibility
For negotiation
For it To be Martyred
Martyred fancy word for
Viciously unjustly
Slaughtered
Grrrr oooo oowwww
she said in a high pitch whisimical
   tone
if from a brass instrument
Grow wild!!
Like unruly unwanted vines
Be un domes ticated.
She said like some cool dude during
   the Black power movement
her eyes large and feral
In an opera like voice she sang,
Grow n b
Untamed like knots in beautiful
   nappy girls hair
After her braids have been taken out
   and she went straight to bed
Have: Tenacity
Tenacity she, I giggled like children
   then recited like robots the
   following:Tenacity and the related
   adjective tenacious are derived
   from the Latin tenax, to "hold
   fast," and from tenere, "to hold."
   Both words are often used to
   refer to a person who doesn't give
   up. Think of how a person would
   tenaciously hold on to the edge of
   a cliff and the tenacity with which
   he would do this.
I whispered to this deformed infant
Roam the earth as a humble God
I am your solider, general
Your GPS nagavitational system
I'm at your disposal
I'm here to give you manure
But who will remember your name?
Does gradios schemes and pictures
   on a box
Flashing pictures
Mimicking moments

Representing you
Mili seconds fractions of stories
It took you maybe 40 years to live
10 years to write
And a month to be published
How many nights
We're you up alone?
This was your debut
The kitchen table was your stage
Moon beams
Spilling on
Tear soaked empty
empty Pages
Pain
This is your moment
Action!!
Colorful head scarf
Unattractively adorned your head
Like a misleading crown
Or we're you born a queen
At the end of the day.. Who remembers you. Not your name?
Your struggle not your fame?
Do they remember the glitter or the courageousness of you sharing your shame?
No standing ovations
At the end of your play
Were they not entertained
I know you bowed deeply when you exited this stage

Ive been dreaming
Of heaven n hell
simultaneously
What are you
gonna do with the fire, Prometheus?
He asked me
He believing
Burning myself is inevitable
Not entertained by my evolution
Nor my internal constellation
Nor my personal solar service
I am
MRS.SOL
The fire is my son..
The first thing
I did with the fire
was lit three candles
And two inscents
emerged deeply
into a hot bath and conversated
with Aphrodite in
mirrored waters
I don't play chess
With fire
With match stick men
I Cultivate trustworthiness
I paint with glass blowers
Folly in cement urban
Forests and and pick
Flowers in Fillmoe
    gardens
To adore my nimbus
Of curls
And politic with poets
Im an octagon
I repeat, I do not play
    chess
With fire
and his smoking
    illusions
Im.more of a mario
    paint, mario cart,
textris, sonic the hedge hog type
of chick
I duck hunt
Admire the
Likeness of the water and for
I admire the transparency of
The fires flame and waters (mirrors)
RosettA stone of the soul
I don't wanna win
Every battle
But admire
The brilliance of my sword
My father told me never show
My weapons
Maybe I trust you
Maybe I dont give a fuck
Have I ever shown dependency
I must
Meticulously search
My mind n heart before I
Speak
I must search twice
No one has it all figured out.. Some
    of us can just persuade others we
do..

art by Roger Moore

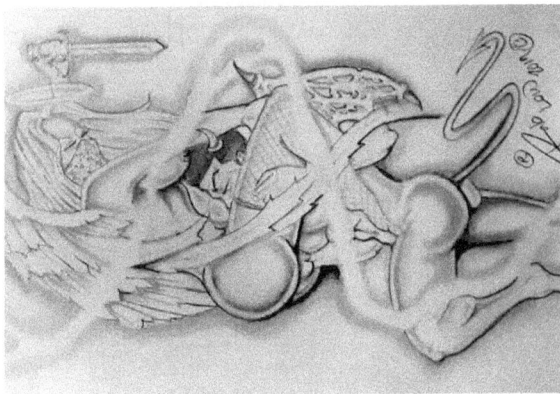

it's more instinctive
than Premeditated
Or some mixture
of an un scaled combination
Whatever the situation
Like braille
I feel it
Minus the hints
Displayed by ya body language
you want a argument
Maybe you like
The intoxication
Of anger
Is he blowing smoke up my ass?
Cause critical thinking
pokes holes in ya theories
Leave em battered n tattered
Like piñatas at a ten year olds birthday party
its not a mystery
I cock in reload
My intellectual ammunition
And laugh at myself
For the satisfaction
I receive form my
Misguided ambition
To make you feel n look
Stupid with plenty of evidence
At the end of it
You have a chip
On your shoulder
And I am the author of this fly ass poem

Inside Out

I read God's message
Like braille
Hard to decipher
Easy to feel
Wish they were
like text messaging
Wish I could request
A closed caption
with My blessings & lessons..
Or maybe jus respond
Different
Internal conversations
Don't know who's talkin
What's Really frustrating
Is this intuition or emotions speaking?
Anger barking
Intellect Interrupting
My emotions while Gods speaking
Desire butts in
Uninvited
to the conversation
And my short term goals
Expand
beyond my souls constellation
Blood diamonds
are sparking…
Desire increase

Poverty is whispering
"A yo' whats up with Trice"
My activism being bullied
I thought,
"I was no rookie"
Fallin victim Animals cruelty
Mink cape..
Looks fly on my back
This vintage bitch!
He'd been dead a long time ago
Now he lives on my back
A yo.. So what? I didn't slaughter his ass
The demons are whispering
Secrets in his semen
My ego screamin "Yacht Dreamin"
Boat shoes with inflated egos
While we meditated
Poverty stagnates our egos
Marginalize our imagination
All the while God sends messages
Via braille
Hard to decipher
Easy to feel
And who has the ability 2 listen
Estranged to trophies
Hidden behind the skin

I don't think
For Mi Yao Mi Yao

I hate you Harrison
I prayed not to hate you
I lay prisoner
Awake in a world with
No bars
To four expanding walls
In between elementary school hours
I seen her face shatter
As another little girl hugged
Her daddy after receiving her diploma
I took the most beautiful picture
I caught her smiling
As I she met my eyes
In the audience
I removed my pain and smiled bak
She tucked her pain
In her back pack
She wraps her Asian eyes
Around
This equation
Two BLACK FEMALES
Fending 4 themselves
I argue with
Other Black women
Whose unacknowledged
support system
Can endure the earthquake
Of single mother hood
They have been oppressed into
Meek silence
And awarded themselves metals
For bravery
We are not equal
I have not
Grown accustom to
MALE PRIVLEGDE
I CANT EVEN EXCUSE THE
    WHITE MAN,
FOR OFFENDING ME
OPPRSSING ME
IVE BEEN STEP ON SO MUCH
BY THE SINGLE BLACK
    FATHERLESS
BLACK MAN
I HAVE AN ADVENTURE STorY
WITH MORE TWIST N TURNS
    THAN HUCKLE BERRY FIN
YEA TOM SAWYER
I Accept lower paying jobs
Because I do
NOT have your support
System to work
Jobs
I have missed radio shows
Had to forfeit opportunities for self
    enhancement
I should have won the Olympics
Long distance race
Cause I have taken care
Of your child for
Going on 8 years
Alone
I thought I was above hate
I even forgave my father for killing my
    mother
But you I want to suffer……
I will continue to teach my daughter
to not endure oppression with a pretty
    smile
she will too stand up and fight back

art by Roger Moore

JUST WRITE A POEM
*HAPPY BELATED BIRTHDAY BOBBY SEAL AND
HAPPY BIRTHDAY BLACK PANTHERS
REST IN PEACE
TO ANY ONE SLAIN ON the BLACK PANTHERS BIRTHDAY
NAMELY THOSE WHO DIED IN EAST OAKLAND
INSPIRED BY: COMMUNITY, EAST OAKLAND
THIS IS A FACTUAL POEM*

you are dying so close to me
we WISH "peace" before we part
we aint fuckin, HELL NAH..
(EVIL PEOPLE ALWAYS SPREAD
 TREACHEROUS LIES)
these my niggaz..
REAL STREET SOLIDERS
I'm the ghetto poet sliding
thru urban war concrete streets
I saluted my niggaz that survive
the Penitentiary
School of Hard Knocks
YOU HAVE TWO PHDS
THEY CALL YO GHETTO WIFE A
 RAT
BUT SHE AIGHT WITH ME
actually she check a bitch
at the store for me
slid my daughter a dolla
I LOVE HOW YALL
WORKING TOGTHER
TO TAKE CARE OR YOUR
 DAUGHTER...
DESPITE YOUR SEPERATION....
REAL NIGGAZ PLEASE STAND
 UP...
CAUSE I KNOW HELLA YALL
THAT HAVE YOUR WOMANS
 BACK
EVERYTHING GOOD YALL
GOES UNNOTIED CAUSE YOUR
A(BLACK)
YOUR ONLY ACKNOWLEGEDED
AFTER YOU ARE SHOT IN THE
 BACK
PEOPLE RARELY EVER
LITE CANDLES
OR BUY YOU
ROSES WHEN YOUR ALIVE
SLIDE THRU TONIGHT
LETS BLOW A CHOP
CAUSE AROUND
THE CORNER
THEY BLEW A COP
LAST NIGHT
BULLETS HAVE NO NAME ON IT
SO IF I CATCH ONE
WHEN YOU LOOKIN
AT THE Sky
KNEW I FINALLY FLEW
THEN WAS ESCORTED
IN A CINDERELLA CHARRIOTT
TO MEET GOD
I promise you
I'll look out for you
JUST PROMISE ME THE SAME
cause I'm sure if you caught a Bullet
Youd go there too
LITE A CANDLE
REMINISE ON DAYS THAT WERE
BETTER
AS THE CIGARETTE
SMOKE BLOWS TO THE SKY
I know your TRUE STORIES
YOUR HISTORY
I BELIEVE IN THE BLACK
 WOMAN

CHILD
AND MAN
TOGETHER LIVING PEACEFULLY
WITH OUR OWN AMENTIES
WITH THE RIGHT TO REFUSE
SERVICE TO THE UNRIGHTEOUS
life has been so hard
i know the only option you have is
TO SURVIVE UNTIL
WE DIE
I KNOW YOU ARE RESTING IN PEACE
YOUR SKIN
WAS
Spiritually Sewned by the
THOUGHT AND BEAUTIFUL IMAGINATION of GOD
In Oakland Caifornia
EAST OAKLAND NAMELY
OH YEA RIP TO THE LITTLE GIRL THAT WAS MURDERED AT EAST MONTE MALL.. I KNOW YOU GOT YOUR WINGS... I KNOW I KNOW YOU.. I JUST WISH I COULD SEE YOU AGAIN AFTER ME AND MY DAUGHTER HOP OF THE BUS AGAIN..

art by Roger Moore

Dear Rapper
he got the mind of a slave
a whip to match it
sell black pussy
jus like the slave masters
then yell Black lives matter
a temper inflamed
no integrity or tactic
With his actions
below average
up to the plate with no bat bruh
wanna make a muffins
with no batter
high risk dick
if she thick
no will never be the answer
a dangerous mind
his brain
a vehicle going 100 mph
with no passengers
he's like a mime
a bad actor
he moving his hands passionately
but ain't saying shit
so it don't matter
reminds me of the gladiators
hella fans
an arena
cheering on violence
coming to watch you loose bruh
a pool pit for proud losers
ignorance seducers
wanna tell you the measurements
but ain't use the ruler

Billie Holiday's Rare Fruits
Now stain concrete streets
Wearing jordans n timberland boots
We have quaters of the truth
The offense has the ball
With 10 seconds to shoot
Most of our teachers
are Courtside
Taught just to Root
Others judge the
Game by birds eye view
I been stop looking to them
4 answers
Preoccupied
with magnifying glasses
Going over the manuscript
The cheerleaders
Are scantily clad
One wind blow from being
exotic dancers
Distracting the minds
Of the chancellor
The ghetto has
Fan clubs
They admire us so much
They redecorate our communities
With wholefoods n irish pubs
And cupid shuffle
The under ground economists
Into cell blocks
A man, a beautiful
A fancy maN, Tall

Very attractive
Dark skin
he was born with a tan
With Jamaican accent
a neat crease in his pants
Fancy pants
man
beautiful dark skin
Asked me..
Then asked me
To ask you are we
Afraid of peace?
I couldn't answer..
Distracted by
my internal answer
My instinct
To speak the truth..
But more importantly
I was more curious about
My truths root.
So I told him ill
Ill call him back
Yes.. I'm afraid of peace
afraid of being a coward
Afraid of Not being respected
By people who I say dont matter
I rather be a barbaric mad hatter
Billy Holidays rare fruit
Thinks a whole bunch of shit
Especially about
truths that make them feel
Venerable

Big stray men
Talking
Shards of glass
Never choking
Mothers worry
Out weighs
Her prayers
on the scale
God cashes in faith
But wraps an invisible
Halo around
These stray men
From prayers
Hummed by grandmothers
25 years ago
bended knees
On wooden floors
Of paid for houses
Boys that snuck colorful candy
From glass dishes on
Wooden Bear clawed coffee tables before dinner
Boys exchanging their innocence
For thrill outside the poolpit
Before
Conjuring experience
To appraise their values
Sweet faced chocolate boys
That thought their faces were just dirt
Wrestle with flesh
Wrestle with spirit

Be strong
For Andrea Smith

Be weak
Cry
Laugh
Reminisce
God parted the sky
Like we do
When we part our daughters hair
Pretty Blacks girls hair..
And shifted planets
That resemble
Colorful knockers
In little pretty Black girls
Hair bins
To make way for
The golden chariot
Drawn by three
chocolate brown
winged regal horses
Star dust swirls
Clarinets
Echo
From heaven
Into the ionosphere
cosmic glitter illuminates
N
Swirls around her room
Settling on the floor
Like a like
Luminous carpet
Her ancient ancestor
Exits the chariot
Adorned in royal purple African silk
To deliver her wings
Your an angel now
Living eternal life n peace

I'm not gonna
Strain a muscle flexion
On ya niggaz
U a run on sentence
Ain't no use
Of correcting u niggaz
I know where you live
Post office, envelope
N stamps
I'm not addressing you Nigga
False bravado
U a broke dope boy
Can't flip coke boy
No hope boy
Tried ya hand at pimp
Now you gotta pregnant
Hoe boy
No bueno
Oh boy
Career couch surfer
Call you potty
Mouth
You lick the Ass
Of bops
Smoking weed
Don't suppress
The validity of
These thoughts
You a hearse
Volunteer dick
In the dirt
5 9 u a smurf
Fight with
Ya bitch
But ain't threw
One bow on the turf
shooting at niggaz
Missing ya target
Only innocent children
Getting merked
Ain't no mistaking identities
But when you a bitch Nigga
It's just friendly fire
Everybody a casual causality

art by Roger Moore

I became a woman that let
Pain dominated her
I kept uplifting myself
Passiveness dominated her
(Good nigger girl)
the truth rolled in my head like
    aimless
marbles,
Be succuessful...
unrooted the roots that
she had planted..
Her friends lol..
tried to decieve her caught up in their
own discression
I fell in love
with her soft smooth skin
light in the winter
Dark in summers she spent in the east
    bay
and abroad...
Melinin that darkened,
with no addatives..
Her BLACK..
Ness..
Divided, multiplied
her settle amongst the out
right raged war
the hood riots...
The gun shots..
she fell in love
with a girl,
she was not gay..
the girl
she was from San Francisco
Fillmoe
Hair thick
Legs thick...
She was taught
to hate herself...
she listened to lauren hill
real shit

she was around real, women men
    children bitches and men the
liars fakes fraud
she was trying to being convinced
    not to
LOVE HERSELF...
But she fell in love with a girl from
    San Francisco
From Fillmoe.
A thick haired
thick legged
thick lipped
light skin chick
who has melannin
who is published....
who dont give a fuck about
a fourth
of a fuck about her loving herself...

art by Roger Moore

Eyes that spread rumors
Before the brain
Can critically
Think
Of a realistic narrative
Negative perspectives
Distort the origins
Of reality
The devil
Aint a white man
In the hood
If women were as
Forgiving to each other
As they were trifling niggaz
Maybe we can have
sisterhoods
Its all distorted
Unrighteous
Rhythm
And 30 year old
Black women
Being aborted
By street terrorist
With no aim
Concealed weapons
On men afraid to show
Emotions
Other than blind
Rage and anger

Women that need more
Protection
Than pepper spray
Everybody
Watching the warriors
Like we aint living
HUNGER GAMES
group mentalities
Women afraid to speak
False
Geopolitical boundaries
Passports
They act like
poverty is a disease
Baby daddies act like Women
Are still in slavery
She supposed to work
Clean cook
be submissive
be blind
pay the bills
raise the kids
be fit
have all the laundry done
hair done
kids hair done
nails done,
On fleek

A bad poets curiosity
Scarred
bit tounges
Recite melodic
pleasantries
To egar ears
Waiting to be adorned
With what they want to hear
The listener wears these words
Like diamond earrings
Telepathic
Earth walkers
Curosity of Death
Linger
On the subconscious
Like a child
Egarly
Awaiting christmas
for moments
To unravel into the present
As religious sinners
Get mad at an individual
Only
critically
thinking
Question
The integrity of THEIR
All knowing
Undivided power having
God
In a world full of evil
Holy rollers wait
For justice to strike
As they cowardly
ONLY
pray
While the women and children
Become prey
Thoughts are like
An intrusive rain storm
The mind
A basin over flowing
Ever flowing
Spilling into rivers
Of concepts
Defying
Reality
Magic floats
upon the stratosphere
Of our being
Waiting for a brave soul
To jump to grab it
Injustice sweeps
The nation
As freedom rings
Poets grow weary of writing poems

Slid to the city
By myself
& The latter
Day saints
All the evil corrupting
Entertaining my folks soul
Blew me the fuck away
I use to hate when
My Nana
Said, baby just pray
I didn't realize
She was exercizing demons
From her wheel chair
Cataracts in her eyes
Her soul
Seen clear
She said
A kitten
Can't fool a cat
Since I'm struggling with
My daughter
Came to the sco to get
    lasanga
My daughter with her father
But I still
Yearn for my momma
Looking at baby my neice
She Taller than me
I look up to her now
Educationally, And physically
Yea I politic
With a Giant
Bust down a beat
Fucked up a poem
On Haight street
Ate 2 snap burgers
While we plotting to build
This thing up like we Nat Turner
Aye, Damn
I seen Toni Morrison
Died on the news
I was so embarrassed
When reading her words

I was stripped naked
With the Blues.
Today my cousins birthday
I felt it in air
I have so many in heaven
I'm good down here

art by Roger Moore

The rose ain't violent
The thorn is
What's mainie
Is that bitch is doormat
Unprovoked
Jus don't pick it
I jus wanna bounce out
Wicked
Illuminious vampire grill
With a few mill tickets
On some viva la pobre shit
Build houses with out
Class,
Teach my ghetto philosophy
That my black ass got outta
Class, critical thinking
I'm not materialistic but ima
Be rockn a vintage mink n
No more Public housing
Or public speaking
It's not they business
What we thinking
I just wanna be in position
To free my peeps
Build a community for single mothers raising
Children alone ,
Bee so dope they find a husban
That honor their commitment
A king and queen on the thrown
Nobody do it on they own
Invest in the youth
Tell them the truth
Ain't no Santa clause
And if a white man give you something
Leave it alone
Bail real niggas outta prison
Change some laws
If they bite we bite back
Word to jaws

You foul
I'ma keep this one tucked
Ill rather masterbate
Than have to close my eyes
to visualize a real nigga
To get my nut..
When we should be making Crazy love
U Wanna kill a niggA fa looking @ me
Crying
Exhausting lazy love
We high off each other
emotionally draining
Im too tired to make it to the club …
Spiritual love
Third ending
I wanna to score
We was dope
Face time
But the connection
Poor
You couldve been
my little slut
But you wanted more
I've been running from relationships
Hiding and not claimin niggaz
I thought you was worth it
I was on super cupcake
nerd, love potion, Slow motion
We talked about getting married
It's kind of scary
I always talk a good ass game
Run it to a nigga
Like you niggaz got grades
Teacher shit
You get An A
But you maintain it
I mentally motivate my niggaz
But with you
I really mean that shit
Our relationship
I prematurely aborted
I can't give you a piece of me
Im not a fraction or proportion
My feelings
Are beautiful
My origins are gorgeous
Not to be dishonored
Down played, manipulated or distorted
If you want a bitch to shut
Up
You should knock a MUTE
One you can disrespect
Knock one with no self-esteem boo…
Im naturally hyper
Why spite me?!
You get me emotional and hyphy
My little Grinch heart had grew in sizing
Im not your opponent
It's alright tho,
Listen to them niggaz
And pay a white man to tell you exactly
What I told you bro
You under mind me you have perfect timing
You kick me
while I was already down
I thought you would have
integrity when we are fighting

God ain't no mutha
fuckin
white man in the sky
He's an Author
A poet
He Writes poems and
Allows people to finish them off
I was just a character added to Patricias poem
Pat 7 verse 18
See she was 18 in July
When. I was written
Martrice 7 verse 1
San Francisco
Summer
Cold morning foggy
Weather predictions say
With a chance of sprinkling
The birds were chirping
A few dogs were barking
It's cold in San Francisco's
Summer's
Martrice will be cold
Her mother's mirror reflection
The stars revealed
An illumnious lion
She will be a beast
A lioness
A fiery butterfly
With flaming maps
As her wings
matriarchal
Opposites n harmony
See told you...

My soul died
11 hundred times
Damn it's fucked up
Man they said a cat
Has only 9 lives
The beast is reincarnated
With matriarch tendencies
To do more than survive
Rest In Peace Dee
Thru Tiny and Tibu
You thrive
I in Tiny words man
I feel no moe
Feel moe key holder
But I'm busting in the
Back doe
It's Feel Moe Africa
But, Gentrification In Feel Moe
Damn it's been snowing
Rest In Peace to Snow
N God
How ??
We just previously
laid down a bright Fillmoe star
Backs a Feel Moe
Damn it's been sad
in Fillmoe
Rest In Peace to Monz Suns
And Lil Lebo
My soul cries when my Sistas n Brothas die

This Lil Big Ass
Poem
Hurt my soul
I don't even know if my
Sistar is 40 years
Old?!?
Dee ain't no
Got Damn restin!
With her daughter
Resisting! Applying hella
Pressure on they neck in
Lost the place in San Francisco
Cause
They gentrifications wrecklesss
I know when a warrior cry
I hate when my big invincible ass
Warrior cry
I could feel the pain in her
She tryna get our
Women n men out this slave system
We kinda ghetto
We Blaze different
Amaze the system
Gorilla
poets
In the building
I hope you looking down from heaven
With my momma, two cousins, my
    nana
Like yea they up on it
Tiny is Mutha Fuckin Tired
Of being reincarnated
Birthing babies
Look Momma Dee
We made it
But they still got that slaveship
You have a grandson and
    granddaughter
That's truly amazing
A whole fuckin tribe that's
The way it's lookin
Now mAn, it sounds like revelations
I'm hyphy but not impatient
I hate the bAttlefield
But we about to blaze it
I forfeit battles to win the war
I have stories untold
I'm a writer
You published me, I'm In tilted
To your love you graces
Aye you seen poor magazine rockin
Building houses on Mac Aurthur ??
People
So when I invested my words in you
You should know
They don't experie
I go back with Annie yu
I also had a type writer

Didn't know we was baby sharks
Swimming up stream
We petted the guppies
But the blood called us
To the see
Blind I
Cut myself on my own teeth
You couldn't pay me to think
A shark did this to me

art by Tristen Hornstein

Did I win?
I mean I provide closed captioning
I took acting classes
I'm not acting
DID I WIN
I got my natural ass , and titties
They told me,
Stand. Up..
Didn't tell me about the tumbles...
Rest I ln peace to my friends,
Aye, bruh..,...
Did I win
I wasn't lookin
At the score board
I'm an investigation journalist
Sis,.... DID I WIN
Cause I ain't sold no pussie
Id.rather DIE..
The way God is aligned
With divine timing
Gloria Yamato
Did I win?
WhTs yo perspective
Objective
Did wine brand kick a peigon
Ever get married
What's
HER STORY,,?
Did we win??
It's windy..

My broken prom queen crown
Lay in a cocouphany of jewelry
Daughter lay awake,
I n the bath
Hot water running
My mind afloat
I'm
Writing a poem
Organic cigarette in my mouth
With a silver plated crown upon my head
I made it to another year
By the hair
Of my chinny
Mutha fuckin
chin
Ive received more Poems from
street soliders
Than I can remember
We fight 2 not
be human
Fruit
Dangling from trees
Rest in peace to those
Black Bodies
That were just recently
Found
Decorating trees
Rest in peace to the
Women, children and men
Died
Fighting the Corona disease
What a fuckin year. Happy birthday to me

Be Like Bat Girl
For: Tristen

Look baby
Look
Look outside
It's
Halloween
Out side
You have many enemies
Like bat man
Look you a bat girl,
You all Black girl
In all black suit
You a Bat girl
Be sweet.
Vanilla or chocolate
Something you tried before
At
an ice
cream parlour
Looking thru the telescope
Not the collide a scope
In time when you
Rich, look like yo broke
Everything that glitters
Catch MOST attention
Glitter ain't Gold
Diamonds glitter
It's a diamond up in ya
Soul
Take a care of that!
It don't matter
what sparkles
Is yo soul
Eat ya dinner
Take a bath
Brush ya teeth
Wash ya face
Again..
Read a book
Be relaxed
Be like Bat Girl

Be polite
Listen more
than you talk
Take people to heaven
Not Hell
Stay up out people's faces
Keep a safe distance
Wash your hands
And your Bat girl face
When you enter a house.
Fuck that Rona
Love, yo momma

art by Tristen Hornstein

I am the artist
Paint the peremiter
Of my body
Yeilding yellows
I stretch halos
To protect my
Spirit from
Them boys
They, Deadly
My brother man man
and I was wondering
Why the police stopped us. .
We was wondering what fuckin
Justification
Did they have to convince themselves
    we
We're criminals
I wonder what was that mutha fuckin
Officers
Internal dialogue
And
I a social doctor
Diagnosed
That mutha Fucka a racist
They had no reason to
Racially profile is and have all of there
    weapons drawn .when we had
    not broken
The law
Why did they call .everyfuckin cop in
    the vacinity
Why were all of there guns drawn
Why are they so afraid of us
Brown and Black Bodies
Shell spirits
Have ancestors that whisper to trees
And know ancient. Secretes your
    history
Can't hear my God's voice
Out deseased are spiritual
Tour guides.we chant with babies
Unborn... Before they arrive
The officer yelled,
With a blood hungry lust in his voice
Anxious..…... anxiously yelled
throw your keys out of the window....
Get out the vehicle.with your hands
    up
20 mental
Health issue
having white supremacists boys in
Blued
Guns
Drawn
Don't turn around... He didn't allow
    for us to look at them
I have exited .
Auto piolet
Hyper trauma
Safeguard activated
I'm
Triggered
They are trigger happy. .
My ex co worker is screaming.
It's my turn,
To exit the car
This is yet another stage
Action .....
Do not turn around
The same blood curling voice
Repeated to me
Put your hands up.
Get
On
the
I follow instructions
Like a script written for me
This ain't no dress rehearsal.
I've been here before
It's action....
She has a weapon!!! An officer
    screamed
Action.
No you do

art by Tristen Hornstein

You tell
Me when the war is
Over
Yall
Act like it's
Just begun
Black infant mortality
Is the highest one
Black women
Are most likely to be slain
By police or domestic violence
pick one
Our sons sisters daughters
Mothers brothers aunties uncles
Aunts friends and foes
Blood runs thru American history
A steady stream pouring into
The mouth of a waterfall
Popular poets
Protest
For more popular causes
Fake activist
Are activated
Trying to secure a spot
In history books
The dishonourable
Is on honor roll
While I fly thru
The bay bridge toll
To return to my native land
Indisputable indestructible integrity
Intact illuminious
While my daughter
Draws Ill illustrations
Ready for publication
I don't beg yo Parton
For spippin
Red wine, beer and or Duce,
    Hennessy or patron
Weed so good make my lips
To heavy for proper enunciation of
    words
Oh my she's, I'm absurd

As I go live
shuckin and jivin
All the while wallowing in
Wilderness
I throw touch downs
And incomplete passes
In
concrete jungles
Ghetto prom queen
EBt princess
While y'all say you from
The hood and
More classist
Than white supremacist
Marganilized
By the spiritually
Maligned
I'm a go rella
Activist
Passing out
Solar lights to
The homeless
Bottled watered
For the hot
Hot Cheetos
For the free
If a little black kid
Is at the corner
Store counting
Out change in front
Of me
Slide my ebt
This is for
Those that barter
With those
That refuse
To be ghetto martyrs
People that repaint
Perimeters of social status
People that
Make being a dope
Spirit a habit
and stretch

Boundaries bound
To keep us in
Socail and spiritual
captivity
This is for the people
Whose votes wasn't
Counted and those
Who didn't vote
Those who
Transform crap
Games on the block
Into chess
Those
Who know the
Beauty of their dreams
And manifest them like whodinni
For those whose words are better
Than silver and gold
For the mutes
With voices
That fear hold them
Hostage
that don't
Have the courage
To speak up
For those whose
Feet slide
And gig
To the rythemic beat
Of the status quo
The far fetch and I'm between
For those that don't know
Why I wrote this poem

Bella Martrice
AUTHOR

Roger Moore
ARTIST

www.ingramcontent.com/pod-product-compliance
Lightning Source LLC
Chambersburg PA
CBHW031423160426
43196CB00008B/1023